From O to Snow

From O to Snow

Kate Marshall Flaherty
Deborah Panko
Donna Langevin

Hidden Brook Press

First Edition

Hidden Brook Press
www.HiddenBrookPress.com
writers@HiddenBrookPress.com

Copyright © 2010 authors

All rights for poems revert to the author. All rights for book, layout and design remain with Hidden Brook Press. No part of this book may be reproduced except by a reviewer who may quote brief passages in a review. The use of any part of this publication reproduced, transmitted in any form or by any means, electronic, mechanical, photocopied, recorded or otherwise stored in a retrieval system without prior written consent of the publisher is an infringement of the copyright law.

From O to Snow
by Kate Marshall Flaherty, Deborah Panko, Donna Langevin

Layout and Design – Richard M. Grove
Cover Design – Richard M. Grove
Cover Photograph – Ron Cole
Author Photograph on back cover – Thane Ladner
Inside bio picture of authors p. 90 – Thane Ladner
Inside Section Art:
   - The Sound of An O – Painting by Bernadette Peets
   - Assumptions – Hummingbird quilt bought at silent auction - quilter unknown
   - So Many Words for Snow – The snowflake was photographed by Ron Cole and crocheted by his mother, Mary Cole.

Typeset in Times New Roman

Printed and bound in Canada

Library and Archives Canada Cataloguing in Publication

Flaherty, Kate Marshall, 1962-
    From O to snow / Kate Marshall Flaherty, Deborah Panko, Donna Langevin.

Poems.
ISBN 978-1-897475-62-1

    1. Canadian poetry (English)--21st century. I. Panko, Deborah, 1951- II. Langevin, Donna III. Title.

PS8611.L25F76 2010   C811'.608   C2010-906819-X

From O to Snow

From O to Snow: a poetic collage from quilts, moqui balls, war memorials, hummingbirds, to an old lady in Cuba to the Virgin Mary stashed somewhere in between. How on earth did our three wildly different manuscripts come to dwell together under the same book cover roof? What unites this mélange?
 Obviously the answer isn't a commonalty of subject matter or style. No, it's something much more fundamental that springs from our lives, a shared commitment to poetry, which brings our work together.
 Kate Marshall-Flaherty and Donna Langevin share a long history of work-shopping at the Artbar Poetry Workshops. Donna Langevin and Deborah Panko met in Cuba in 2007, where they work-shopped and gave readings with other members of the Canada Cuba Literary Alliance (CCLA). When they got home, Donna introduced Deb to Katie at one of the Artbar workshops. Then, as luck would have it, we all turned up in "Not a Muse," an anthology of international women's poetry edited by Kate Rogers and Viki Holmes which explores the lives of women in their

diverse roles such as Creator, Archetype, Freedom Fighter and Myth Maker. As even better luck smiled on us, we came together again as featured readers one magical evening at the "Meet at 66 East Fine Dessert Lounge" in Cobourg. Good things often arrive in threes. Our third stroke of good luck was that Richard Grove, who had published each of our first books with Hidden Brook Press, was so captivated by our reading that he decided there and then to do an anthology featuring all three of us. Thus *From O to Snow* was born—a single anthology birthed by three different muses who all draw their inspiration from the single fountain of poetry.

Vive la Difference! A bouquet is made up of various flowers, a forest of many trees and a party is a bowl of mixed nuts. Let's make no assumptions. O might mean Oh, Ooooo, Oops, Oww, or oh-oh. Enjoy the wonder of life's variety show in this eclectic collection!

The authors:
Kate Marshall Flaherty,
Deborah Panko and
Donna Langevin

Table of Contents

The Sound of An O
by Kate Marshall Flaherty

– Breath Chorus – *p. 5*
– Flight – *p .6*
– Gemini – *p. 7*
– Judgment Dream – *p. 8*
– Bubble Bath – *p. 9*
– Metta – *p. 10*
– Oh – *p. 11*
– Minnow – *p. 12*
– Anti-Aunt – *p. 13*
– Attention – *p. 14*
– National Geographic Photo – *p. 15*
– Pre Dawn – *p. 16*
– Meditation on a Small Space – *p. 17*
– Skipping Stones – *p. 18*
– When the Body Says No – *p. 19*
– Permission to Grieve – *p. 20*
– Sanctuary Sunday – *p. 22*
– Circle – *p. 24*
– Mystic – *p. 25*

Assumptions
by Deborah Panko

– History Lesson – *p. 31*
– Faith Bought in a Crystal Shop – *p. 33*
– Aristocrats – *p. 34*
– Judgment Day – *p. 35*
– Dorothy Winter's Quilt – *p. 36*
– Taxi Lesson – *p. 38*
– Hummingbird – *p. 40*
– Non-negotiable Lifestyle – *p. 42*
– Water Table … Turning – *p. 44*
– Cowbird – *p. 46*
– Public Servant – *p. 48*
– Named – *p. 50*
– An Assumption within an Assumption – *p. 51*
– Ron – *p. 52*
– Desire – *p. 53*
– Unspoken – *p. 54*
– Framework – *p. 55*

So Many Words for Snow
by Donna Langevin

- Typos – *p. 61*
- Hot Chocolate Rag – *p. 62*
- Our Igloo – *p. 63*
- The Many Holes in a Snowflake – *p. 65*
- Just Wondering – *p. 66*
- A Snowflake – *p. 67*
- Arachne's Second Contest – *p. 68*
- The Inquisitor of Snow – *p. 69*
- Mai in December – *p. 70*
- Unfolding – *p. 71*
- My Address Book – *p. 72*
- The Ice Bee – *p. 73*
- Icewine – *p. 75*
- The Alibis of Angels – *p. 76*
- The Best Way to Eat a Snowflake – *p. 78*
- Snow – *p. 79*
- A Little White Music – *p. 80*
- Blue – *p. 81*
- Old Stripper Snow – *p. 82*
- April Snowman – *p. 83*
- Distances – *p. 84*
- Snowdrops – *p. 85*
- Hydrangeas – *p. 85*
- Hydrangeazzzzzz – *p. 85*
- Today People Are Snowing on Cabbagetown – *p. 86*

The Sound Of An O
Kate Marshall Flaherty

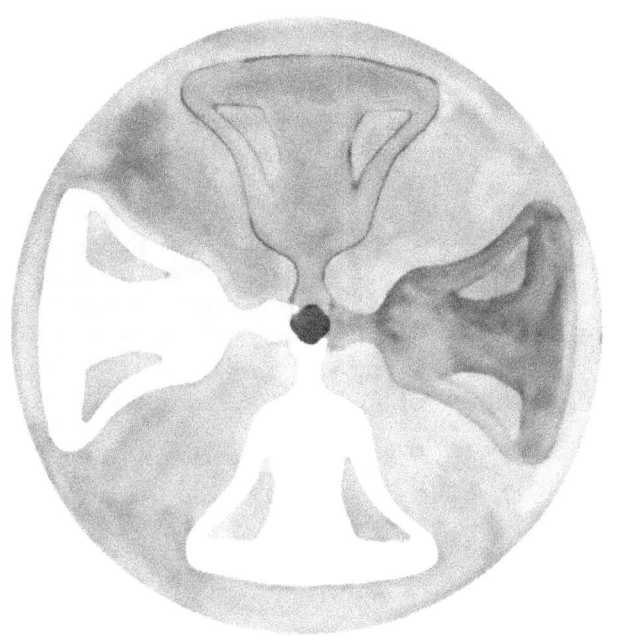

For my family,
John, Annie, Gabriel and Locky:
Oh what fun, what challenges, what gifts,
what music, what wisdom,
what spirit,
what a wonderful blessing
to have you four in my life!
You are my angels.

Breath Chorus

Draw in a deep intake of breath—
then consider the whispered exhalation
across the damp reed of the voice box.

What an instrument, this wonderful wind pipe!

Listening to my own notes
fluting through the skin drum of my tympanum,
I wonder what I sound like, outside myself?

What does my hoarse speech sound like to you?

I drink warm honey
and try again, repeat, say once more
a chorus of consonants and odd vowels

and then—be silent.

Listen to me
listening to myself,
breath making waves of sound,

and I will try again, repeat myself,
say once more
a chorus of consonants and odd vowels.

A gentle striking of air on vocal chords equals voice.
A gentle striking of air on the eardrum equals hearing.

A gentle unstruck heart, open to air, sound,
silence   equals listening.

Flight

What matters, then, is that Annie is leaving
for Atlantic shores.
Waves of the ways we'll miss
her mentoring amid mayhem,
the mirth in her eyes.

We are left behind—
the boys and I—
Kings of Siam without their Anna.
The lost boys without their Wendy,
clapping madly because they still believe in fairies.
    The magic when a sister pays attention.

What matters is the shadow she'll leave behind.
She'll not be around to mend
the tears, to stitch things back on, to tell them stories
and remind them, "lovelier thoughts, boys, and up you'll go!"
    They leave the window open.

She will be both here and there,
    like growing up.
    A space she leaves for them to step into.

Gemini

Twins, it figures—
Lady Laudable and Mistress My-way.

One a gentle guru whispering of radiance, one a sumo
wrestling the remote right out of your freakin' hand.

The bright mother writes a love note on your boiled egg,
the other stays up nights repeating the beads of your penance.

Our sunny sister lets you play hooky and ferry to the island,
her shadier sibling cancels movie night after a fib and cover-up.

Princess of spontaneous picnics and parties,
mirrors her kin, Duchess of Directives and to-do lists.

O, Geminorum, our two-sided constellation, always
coming up sudden, like spring.

We never know, after the green rain,
what will sprout from the muck—

morning glories in the surprise slant of sunlight,
or poisonweed in the dusk of deadly nightshade?

Judgment Dream

You are being funneled into a spacious stadium,
alone in a crowd of silent and backward-gazing others.

The enormous spotlight strobes,
points down from the night sky onto a strange opaque gate.

You feel whimpering confessions bubbling up in your throat,
caught part way with sticky half-truths, big as gob-stoppers.

You choke. The lights are harsh and interrogating
and you feel like a bug on a microscope slide.

Eventually you arrive at a door like an airport metal detector—
or is it a lie detector? You can't stop the shivers.

Too frightened to cross the threshold, you look back
at the stony faces and barely catch your breath.

Something propels you towards the door frame. You stand
in blinding brightness—a billion pinpricks of light.

And all your steely armor, your ragged screams,
your thick and viscous lies, all your searing rage

your piss-furies and deep and dank depressions
get nuked in this portal of light.

They fly from you like chaff in the wind;
bits of shattered gems dispersing in the clear.

Bubble Bath

The best place *not* to think is a hot bath
where you soak in the fragrant marinade
and soften until poisons leach out.

They float outside your body
then swirl down the drain—
thoughts attaching to bubbles like little round horses
charging out of you—
racing down the slippery tunnel,
and popping somewhere under the earth!

Metta
(the practice of loving kindness)

It smells like candle-warmed lavender oil,
this soft slide of hands
smoothing over the spine's protrusions.

Its colour is as faint
as cinnamon cookie stains on parchment,
and it tastes like amber honey on a spoon.

It opens up and laughs out loud,
sometimes leaving a moist trail.

Kindness often slips in, unexpected,
leaving a glowing.

Like this morning,
someone's metta rested its head on my shoulder
longer than a moment, as if to say,
after everything, "I know. I am here."

Oh!

I had a hard time today
trying to write words for a song—
even red wine didn't help.

I kept thinking of O's—
zero, nothing, nada,
dial tone, dead air.

I saw the shape of mouthing surprise,
an operatic whole note,
the base of a snowman sketch,
goose egg.

I let out a groan of desperation,
but still no lyrics. None.

I doodled on my napkin,
loops of ink like coils on a combine,
and even there I noted cursive vowels: *ooooo*
but no song.
Only holes in three-ring paper.

I had another round,
lifted the glass,
the wine stem stain
a mulberry eclipse on linen.
I orbited my finger on the rim—

Oh the sound:
One long note
               suspended like a halo.

Minnow

Walking past the field to the pond,
I listen to the *!gung !gung* sound of bull frogs,
their throaty professions stopped by the occasional pop
of water as an open-mouthed catfish surfaces.

The smells of bulrushes and brackish pond water
remind me of the bucket of minnows
we forgot in the shed when we were kids.
The smell of silvery bodies in the heat
turned to thick soup that the raccoons tipped over,
scrabbling for crawfish at the bottom.

That's me, darting around the tin bucket—
one of too many bodies in a small container.
Yet all the other swimmers seem happy to zig and mingle,
while I just wish for a pail of my own.

It was always like this:
the cousins laughing in the barn hay
while I wandered out to the pond,
the kids and their dad off to Wonderland
while I cocooned at home by my desk,
the parties of people chattering and clinking drinks
while I sat aside from their circles,

the lonely minnow in a crowded skein,
always looking for escape.

Anti Auntie
> *for Polly*

There's a photo of you
leaning over a ladybug
with our two-year-old—
your once nephew.
One hand rests on his overall'd bum
gently tapping his Pampers,
the other points past the prickly thistles
to something wonderful.

Your eyebrows lift an arc
as round as his small o mouth—
Oh! Oh! Auntie Polly's
fox costume, clown nose and Mama Bear apron!
Enchanted eyes wide with surprise; you
the kid-friendly queen.

This is a rare keepsake.
Polly, no longer my sunny sister-in-law,
my partner's brother's ex—
now an un-relative, and anti-aunt,
the severed branch of the family tree.

I wish I had tended the roots we entwined,
now lost to soil.

I miss you like a ghost limb.

Attention
       all you hibernating seeds, sprouts-to-be,
       nubs and nubbins, furled-up pods
       waiting to swell up in the sun!
       You can now dare to st…st…stutter into spring.
       Stammering *muck muck loam and fecundity*—
       Let's kick start this greening!

Pull the ripcord and
       Pull the rrrip-cord and
             Pull the rrr   rrrr   rrrrrr—
Let's get this garden started!

O! A bud
     a buding
         a-budding knob
             of crocus protrudes:

sprung rhythm
      spring fathoms …

      All you leafy-greens and buds,
      flowerlets and seedlings—
      warm up, unite …
      spring fever forever!

National Geographic Photograph

I see her—
Oh, a human bulrush in a drought,
her breasts shriveled to dry flaps,
a skeleton draped
in a dark sari of skin,
with bangles on her bone wrist—
too young
for the dusty elephant creases
on her knees and elbows.

Through the taut scrim of her eyes
I see a parchment lantern lit
with only a lump of candle left.

She leans into the harsh wind,
        a broken human ladder.

I can't help but remember
the hooded ghost revealing two scrawny
starvelings under his great robe:
want and, *the most dangerous by far, ignorance.*

An echo shuffles down a long corridor, *"Spirit,
I fear you most of all."*

The refugee road stretches long under naked branches,
a stripped tree.

Pre Dawn

The quietest time
is dark morning
when the air is vibrant
with a thick purple blackness,
when I sit at my desk in the softest dark,
still in my flannel night shirt,
warming my hands on a hot mug of tea.
And I stare at everything
in the absence of light.

The quietest time is somewhere
around 5 am, that threshold
of suspended stillness, just before
the birds re-awaken
and start their mounting cacophony
of sweet twitters and twig songs.

Some, who sense this waiting time, will say
the air is purest now,
so breathe it in
before the settled sediments of sound are stirred up
once again. Before the world awakens,

the quietest time
is the surprising shape of an O.
Empty yet full.

Meditation on a small space

That small notch
at the back of a baby's head
base of skull, top of spine—

there's wisdom lodged in that hollow.
The same light that glowed in caves,
illuminated birthings,
burned the slash for new shoots.

Ancient brain stem
since the beginning of time.

Skipping Stones

Ages of banter by the bathtub,
rhyming songs, stories, five finger prayers.
Constant questions and big flat skippers in the sun.

Sometimes she had to wait for answers—
sometimes he'd get lost in thoughts.
The back-and-forth reflections growing slowly silent,
eventually skidding into awkwardness.

Then came contests, criticisms, count-downs.

One day she learned to be silent—
all those stories that made him the hero,
all those stroking sounds at times of suffering,
all those words of encouragement—

Her breath no longer blew him onwards.
It never really did.

When the Body Says No

I'm standing at the ledge
of the dusty chalkboard—
my fingers still dry
from pressed chalk and cursive letters.

I look at my fingers
under strips of fluorescent lights
and canary yellow poster paper
with punctuation marks and classroom Golden Rules.
Max's wooly head rests on the desk in front of me.

The lighting so stark in this moment—
the smell of sun-withered African violets on the sill,
the taste of utter exhaustion
like licking an empty rice bowl.

I am weary.
The kids are pining for summer.

The lights buzz hard, like locusts.
My right fingertips, hand, wrist, shoulder
are numb. Not no-feel numbness,
but a tingling shock –
a toaster shorting out.

I have been stripped right down
to a power cord, tattered and frayed.
My nerve-wires exposed.
they spark and surprise me.

Part of my body sings out in currents,
"STOP
    NOW
        AND
            LISTEN."

Permission to Grieve
    (a tumbling Glosa)

> *one day you finally knew*
> *and you felt the old tug*
> *at the very foundation—*
> *enough—and a wild night*
> *into the world*
>   Mary Oliver, "The Journey"

One day you finally knew—
all those dreams of hostels and hotels,
of garden inns and dusted mansions
were crammed together like lemmings
about to jettison off a cliff.

This morning you wake weeping
feeling the old tug
of your scrabbling dream-family
pull at your ankles
but sleepily you slip off your night sock
and wiggle your bare toes in the warmth.

You remember the lynx at the farm
that gnawed its own femur
at the very foundation,
to free itself from the iron clamp
of the trapper's device.
You recall the crimson dots
left on the snow.

You wonder would you cut off a limb
if it pinned you to the past? Pluck out an eye
if it had seen more than
enough? A wild night
of cabin-dreams and bolted shutters
have left your nightshirt soaked with sweat.
Your eyes are bright this almost-morning.
Some soft lump loose in your throat.

"You stand naked in a sliver of light.
This last nightmare broken
like a fever; beads
of sweat have sloughed off the tough scales of the year.
It is Epiphany.
You take off your night shirt and waken
into the world."

Sanctuary Sunday
for my writing group

"Did you go to church today?" you ask.
I answer, yes, my love
inclining it was a liturgy of sorts.

My sanctuary was sitting by the hearth,
where crackling fire sparked
in a place of insights igniting, a place
of combusting creativity.

My mass was in whispers of wind through fall leaves
that spoke to me
as Spirit breezed through the screen
while I wrote.

The vessel of my body stepped on mossed earth
and stood by a gnarled tree. My thoughts
connected the rings of my life with the circles
exposed by its hacked-off branch;
the wide rings from seasons of abundance
and thin ones from dry spells.
I lifted my limbs in praise
and considered my kinship
with this tree.

I did not do penance,
although I did recall standing atop Takakaw Falls,
feeling I was on eagle's wings
high above the pound of water, so close
to the clouds that the wind lifted my spirits
to a place I ache to return to.

There were no recitations
of prayers from a psalter today,
but I let flow blood from heart to hand,
from pen-ink to paper,
and let a little gratitude spill out in circles
of cursive onto white.

I read a new verse and chapter—the gospel
of groundwater. We listened to its purging burble
as it washed away yesterday's residue.

Circle

I heard You calling me
in the night—
you were whispering my spirit name
like a gentle breeze
returning

All my shimmering dream-leaves
turned towards you, Beloved

I worry
the wars of this world
have worn out your name
and I am sorry for this
because I want to sing Alleluia
to you, Jesu, Beloved One

but I will still know you
in the silence
that wraps around my heart
Oh!

Mystic

Inside this stone cathedral
where even silence
echoes in polished marble—
the quietest thing
is the after-chanting
when the sisters' voices
have ceased

and harmonies hover
in their holy corridors.

When stillness settles like fine dust
on a monument,
when wooden benches soak up slanting
stained-glass light,
when sound vibrations penetrate
deep into cells, and even deeper
between them,
then is there space
for the quietest thing.

Listen—
beyond the rhythm of blood,
beneath the waves of breath,

there is a silent radiance
in the core of your heart
so still
so soundless
no-thing

it is
like listening
to the sun.

Assumptions
Deborah Panko

For my sister, Cher
keeper of the hearth.

History Lesson

I open the hardcover book
and a bird flies out,
brown-speckled
flurry of downy feathers.

My fearful heart says
it can't be true, I couldn't be the one
who placed him there,
soft, warm body

pressed into black ink
long since drawn from pen,
like dried autumn leaves
taken back in time,

this bird
both dead and alive,
eternal image in my mind, fixed
at the moment of freeing itself.

There must be between the lines some clue
that can tell you this isn't my fault,
it isn't my intention
to shut desire inside a book's covers.

There must be a reason
for feeling these wings take flight,
for wanting it to happen,
so wanting this to happen.

*Moqui Balls (aka Moki Marbles) are literally "splash" drops of hematite-coated sand and iron (iron meteorites impacting into sand). Slightly magnetic, Moqui Balls (sold in pairs) were believed by some Native American cultures in the Utah area to assist in shamanic journeys and are presently used to heighten psychic abilities, for astral travel, to shield against unwanted psychic influences and with the Third Eye Chakra.

**Faith Bought in a Crystal Shop
in Toronto, Canada
at the End of the 20th Century**

Shamen of southwestern deserts
once held magical moqui balls*,
worn skins a perfect fit,
centered in their palms.

Before men drove hammer to nail - before
life meant purpose and justice trumped intent,
mystics merged stone and grain,
danced for rain. Together

they listened for the far-off canyon's refrain.
With vision clear and strong as a clap of thunder,
they lifted their medicine to the sky;
earth trembled, waters broke, seed pods burst.

Dispassionate now, we see polished rock
the colour of iron,
time held between us, yielding … unyielding
like the wind.

An open hand could meet
this faith let in so long ago,
a faith that prowled the rim's circumference,
wrapped itself 'round their whorled shells,

became the pressure within that bends
fingers over what wants to begin,
a faith that pulled outside in,
a faith that could make sense of it all.

Aristocrats

Fidel says no begging–
Cubans will do it on their own–
yet, as we approach the crowded intersection,
an insistent, female voice …
"por favor, por favor."

If I turn to face her,
I will have to share–
her path, her needs,
my awkward response.
I do as I must do.

She is ancient, tiny,
leaning on a cane
poised at the edge of a drop …
this foot high curb looming before her
a quarter of her height.

"Gracias," she says, as I offer her my arm,
and for this remembered time,
she, as my Baba Yaga,
and I, her chosen Maid of Honour,
meet the risks of a steep descent.

Judgment Day

Cheeks flushed, hands dropped close at her sides
like the chrysalis of a monarch in its body bag
weightless and waiting
our heroine, in death, has achieved
atonement for her gaudy past.

It is the end of La Traviata,
those few still moments of contemplation
when hidden wings
drawn to the light
begin, membrane against membrane, to stir.

"So is it all worth it?" I ask,
turning in my seat to face Margaret,
retired gynecologist
and worldwide observer of birds.
"Life, I mean."

Obliging eyes meet mine,
and, with practiced precision,
the opera lover's mind gives way, shocks us both.
"Just,"
she says,

as our soprano,
rendered modest in gauzy white gown,
opens out arms to mounting applause,
absolution gladly delivered
in the wake of a devilish laugh.

Dorothy Winter's Quilt

She said the one I wanted,
the one hanging on her kitchen wall,
was called Charivari.

From a long-ago-time
of courtly love and honourable intentions,
ten figures come marching in a row,
each in a pointed cap or collared kerchief
to match his tunic, tights and cloth boots.

With bells and beaters,
they are a noisy lot.
The one in purple plays a fiddle,
the one in orange, a flute.
Some have eyes, some have none,
one a moustache but no nose,
one no mouth but a drum.

A distant relative of our remnant, Shivaree–
tin cans tied to a car bumper–
this quilt is a complex of textures
like the one who made it.
Speckled or flecked,
streaked or honeycombed,
each shape is its own delicate pattern,
each severed piece, a final choice,
the centre field holding them all
a bold, blood red.

It is the figure at the far right,
the 11th one who stands out,

his tunic striped like a convict's pyjamas,
left arm stiff, hand gripped at his side,
mouth gaped, waiting for air.
Why they mock him,
why he must pass before them
is unknown,
their ritual absorbing the light
of calm but crooked smiles.

Crossed with even, straight lines,
the mottled, fiery centre
is bordered by vertical bars,
a squadron of rectangles around the square,
each threaded through with a swirl of s's,
Dorothy advancing one stitch at a time.

Three figures with blue faces
are cloaked in forest green,
the same fabric banding the top,
the quilt's sky, and the bottom ...
fertility both in heaven and in hell.

A truer representative
than the artist's lettered signature,
the black spider floats
in the crimson corner at the left.

What Dorothy has woven now hangs
on my dining room wall,
this spirited protest of a captured imagination.

Taxi Lesson

Tired of walking in Havana's hot sun,
unsure of the distance left to go,
we three hail the unmarked taxi,
red-roaring 70's Lada
still up to the task.

The driver's black eyes are smiling:
his five fingers
for our five convertible pesos.
"Si, si, si, entiendo - 17 and H Street."
He understands,

and yes, yes, yes, we share his confidence,
step into the snorting chariot.
Gears grinding, round and round in circles
we race all the other chariots bearing down in
determination, duct tape and deadly fumes.

Brakes pumping, heads throbbing
and it's "No, no, no, not here, not 17H Street,"
as we rummage for dictionary, paper, pen ...
"two different streets ... dos ka-lyes ... croo-the ...
the intersection of ... dye-thee-sye-te—EE—a-che."

Now with even more distance left to go,
our fearful eyes, five fingers and failing words
circle round and round,
looking for the 'and' between 17 and H ...
in Spanish, the letter 'Y'.

Final countdown to the crossroads
and si, si, si - entiendo.
At least I think I do.
The driver is overcharging us
but has wanted to give us our money's worth.

Hummingbird

Native Indian symbol for healing,
hummingbird
pulls north, south, east and west up
into her wings - a blur of looping eights,

hovers for a moment
above pebbled path and dusty shoes,
her nectar-drenched beak
targeting my tie-dyed T-shirt.

We are walking
silently, somewhere
on Mt. Shasta in Southern California
through a garden of iron sculptures,

wartime scenes from Vietnam
visited like stations of the cross–
before me a soldier carried on a stretcher
led by a nurse holding a lamp.

All metal to withstand the heat,
the eroding wind,
these sculptures honour the sacrifice
but mostly call on regret.

Glitter of green wings,
an arrow in slow motion
touches down on the yellow of a creosote bush,
on the impenetrable soldier clinging to life,

circles the rainbow swirls of my summer top,
rounding up fragments of this unfinished story,
then ... leaving our hearts behind
stuck at the altar of heroic humanity,
vanishes into the blue.

Non-negotiable Lifestyle

It happens:
when there's nowhere else to go,
things do seem to come together.

The blinding sunlight,
the coffin opening just a crack,
your peeking in just as we had.

You see in an instant
you too are done with it all ...
the living mysteries.

Only a shadow in this world now
flitting like a moth among flowers–
surface trappings–

you've turned to us,
to what will save you,
to life's eternal blood.

You've met the chosen ones,
we who have abandoned time ...
too dangerous for the dead

or alive, depending on your tastes.
When you do arrive,
cold as your angel in the snow,

when you recognize
the first stage of our dance,
you will know it's true.

In this moment,
you will let it come–
the language before language

from the soft flesh of your neck–
and finally know who you are,
what you have always been.

Water Table ... Turning

On May 15th, 2008,
in the headline story of the National Post,
a new word has been used for
draining a wetland.

The word is easy to miss.
No single quotation marks to set it off,
no comments about its usage,
it blends seamlessly into a report
on the Kearl project in Northern Alberta,
where Imperial Oil/Exxon Mobil Corporation
assumes the land,
turns tar to gold.

Now is the time,
before the word ripens,
to strap the company's oracle
supine on a table turned for better viewing,
to plumb its testes for depth,
weed out screams and howls,
uproot its seed.

The scythe's blade shining paper-thin,
sharp over a distended belly,
eyes growing wide, so wide
they hold this world's entire tragedy,
then protons wilting,
blue black blood leaking the colour of tarsands,

tears dabbed, drool sponged,
and the corporate swamp is ...

de-watered.

The word in the report–
original sin righteously carved into consciousness,
a new word to fertilize the scale, scope
and speed of profits while birthing a dead zone–
is de-watered.

Yet another image in the making,
some new word that can de-fish fish habitat
by means other than fishing,
wriggles at the periphery of this predator's brain,
but for now the words are ...

de-membered.

Cowbird

that part of me I dislike,
that my conscience doesn't accept

says you have no right to be
making your home here

a prairie dweller
who should be riding the backs of buffalo

not laying your eggs in another's nest
leaving parenting to the more industrious ones

your over-sized offspring
eating what is meant for the legitimate.

You thrive on space but here
you displace the ones who belong.

I turned the garden hose on you
pummeling you with my gushing emotions

like I did that squirrel once
running atop a telephone wire

but only after he dared me–
standing on his haunches

asserting it was his backyard, not mine.
I showed him

the punishing waters chasing him
all the way to the road

but not you.
Your alien black eye

rapid wing beats like buckshot
spraying tank top, shorts

I felt pulled
back into my own darkness

like the black dog of depression
its head dipped in mud brown

cowl of adaptability
howl of aggression

your cowbird creaks and bubbles, chucks and glugs
wrapped in a feathered crown

taken up residence
before I even knew what hit me.

Public Servant

As a model for administrators,
the mayor and I
represent two sides of the same raft.

A negotiator
at the Great Lakes round table,
Peter divides the pie into slices:

one wedge
given without debate to fishermen,
a big chunk
swacked with an ax for industry,
flute-crusted piece
for smooth sailing boats,
thin strip
for tiny tots with parents on a sandy beach

and, with a nod to those
hired to honour ecosystems,
a quick perusal
of their research documents:

bacteria levels in sewage,
dead duck counts,
sludge removal costs,
analyses of chemical compounds
altering the composition of egg shells,
the fertility of frogs.

The mayor,
looking upwards to his heaven,
believes in life rafts.

From the bottom of the raft,
face-down in water,
the writer of this poem wonders
what it is like to be a lake
looking at itself.

Named

They took the names we called them by
to help our eyes to see ...
rabbit, rat, chimpanzee,
tiger, bat, bumblebee.

They let us know we'd met somewhere,
shared wind, rain, northern lake ...
monarch, bear, meadowlark,
moose, bullfrog, snake,

then hid away, fled further still.
Light scattered as they flew ...
falcon, shark, whooping crane,
vulture, kangaroo.

If only words could find their way,
lift us from where we lie ...
warbler, whale, elephant,
gorilla, dragonfly.

Haunted voices, this earth's hymn
met by a waxing moon ...
wood thrush, mourning dove, whip-poor-will,
wolf, owl, loon.

An Assumption within an Assumption
(August 15th - the Virgin's Ascent to Heaven)

Mary achieved it, an assumption
granted to the mother of the son of God,

a return after death
to the other side of suffering,

that sought after reward
granted by the translators of all that mattered,

a place as esteemed as that accorded
to everything both known and unknown.

She had performed well,
done her duty in seeing that the seed was sown,

wrapped 'all that mattered'
in swaddling clothes,

watched the seed take root and flourish,
listened as the words grew confident,

fell to her knees
at the inevitable loss.

She was holy too,
just not as important as 'all that mattered'.

In her silence, our assumption ...
that she has been pleased with the results.

Ron

makes me
weak in the knees,
in his night shirt and shorts,
giving that unique perspective
on the state of the world over morning
coffee at the kitchen counter.
Whether from age or from
laughter, I am
first to
sit
down
to wait
as he brings out
his most recent photo
of fuzzy sunflowers leaning
into each other at Bob's organic
farm, and before he goes to do
garbage detail because
it's Friday, he
gathers
me
up
again
and I let him
because we both know when
someone makes you weak in the knees,
like that, you don't want to leave even when
you have to get up now because
the kettle's boiling, and
the sun's out, so
welcome,
like
him,
constant,
these ocean waves
knocking me off my feet ...

Desire

Treat her as an abstract
with drooping shoulders,
a practiced form yet out of reach

feign divine indifference
as if nothing in particular matters
and still you will

wake each morning
to what wants to be there,
knowing she's everywhere

and everything matters.
The ancients say she is god's idea
falling like Lucifer from the stars

a place of danger
to and through
where even the thought of her lies

but when she is breath
pulled from out there
to where you are

sentient,
tangible,
you take her at her word.

Unspoken

This can only be known by you
since you are the only one
I want to walk with
through lived-in rooms
of faded carpets and reading lamps,
to climb deliberately to the top of the stairs,
bend slightly as we step
into a room beyond rooms,
sit knees to chin, palms against
an uneven, patchy concrete floor
damp from a distant earth,
face yet another door
warped with time
that doesn't quite close.

We are alone here,
here where prayers begin,
where you lean into my breathing,
pull at the words I have drawn into myself,
words that keep this last place safe and secret,
where you listen to the timid pace of my heart,
search for the one word
that will allow me to leave.

Framework

Within these words
dark
drawn from the light
ascending
under the noon-day sun

So Many Words For Snow
Donna Langevin

For my sons:

André, my math wizard
who painted a multicoloured snowfall in kindergarten
René, who loves winter sports
James, who transforms snowstorms into music.

Typos

Oh oh I've keyed in "snowfake"

Can a snowflake be fake?

A paper snowflake is a fake

The plastic ones adorning
store windows at Christmas time
are imposters

The knitted ones on my sweater are wooly
and too warm to be genuine

You can't fool me with those crystals
hanging from threads

but ah!   Today's first snowfall—
cool exquisite lace crocheted by angels
    drifting
        lazily
            down

Oh oh I've typed in "slowflake"

Put my typos together
    Here's a tongue twister—
slow snow fake flake

I think I'll quit writing now
and go out for a walk instead
let real flakes not yet disguised
   as metaphors
      land
on my hands and head

Hot Chocolate Rag*
for James

this warm refuge rag
composed
in a New York coffee shop
in the middle of a snowstorm
100 years ago
    steams today
from the keyboard
of my ragster son—

his left hand cupping
the bass chords
    in strict marching time
his right hand pours out
    melody
        rich as dark chocolate
with syncopated cinnamon
and flourishes like whipped cream
while I
    the marshmallow mom
take a break from my blues
two-step
    to the rhythm
and drink in
    his *joie de vivre*
piping-hot from his soul
  while snowflakes dance
    past our windowpanes
and the wind
        whirls and twirls

Our Igloo

will arrive
on your doorstep
beautifully assembled
accompanied by
cheerful polar bears
and the traditional
jellybeans, gumdrops
candy fish and other
gingerbread animals
frolicking in the marzipan snow

Personalize your igloo now
with a name or holiday greeting
The roof accommodates
one line of up to fourteen
characters including spaces
not including mountains
glaciers, icebergs, fiords

The sturdy base
made from wind-resistant cardboard
is fully guaranteed against
cracking, folding, crunching

The hand-iced edible scenery
a unique gift from the Arctic
will be delivered to your address
without you having to lift a finger
harpoon, paddle
or whack a path through a sea
of unwelcome shoppers
salespeople, Inuit

Call now for your fun treat
One igloo can provide dessert for
your entire family and friends
Offers limited
An L.L. Bean exclusive
$59. 95 (excluding shipping and tax)
Delivery within 3 business days
(weather permitting)

The Many Holes in a Snowflake

There are nostrils
mouths and ear-holes
pinholes and peepholes
holes that lead to China
the dikes of Holland
and the levees in New Orleans

There are loopholes like alibis
wounds like bullet holes
or the words in Leonard Cohen's song
"He gave her a flake of his life"

And when the snow sifts down today
I imagine a math wizard adding up
centuries of holes as he tries
to calculate how many zeroes
there are in humanity

So many snowflakes
riddled with shining holes
lovely because of their holes
and because they fall
and we also fall
from grace
and from God
our souls holy, like snowflakes

Just Wondering

If man is made
in the image of God
then is a snowman made
in the image of a snow-god?
If so, does that god have
eyes that burn like coal
a nose like an inquisitive carrot?

Is his nature
frosty
adorable
approachable
or abominable?

Does he stride across the world
from Africa to India to Canada
leaving giant footprints
tell-tale hairs, reportedly changing
shape and names – *Yeti, Big Foot,
Misasqwatomin, Sasquatch*

Or is there a goddess instead
made from Isis-water
fur and bone
snow-stars
or missionary tales?

Does she speak in holy communion wafers
or flakes of falling manna?

Does she give a frozen fig about redemption
when she dies in spring
with sunlight in her pores?

A Snowflake

is so beautiful I don't want
to darn or mend it
pick up holes
   like dropped stitches
     unraveling
        the whole design
to re-knit it tighter
   warmer   fleecier

  pearl plain
    plain purl
cable stitch
      slip stitch
    cross stitch
  witch stitch
   triptych
nothing can compare

with a snowflake
    that can't be made with
knitting needles, crochet hooks
  looms, bobbins, scissors
the hands of a tailor, painter
      seamstress
      spinner
   maker of bridal lace

Arachne's Second Contest*

It was the snowflake
on my windowsill
that really challenged me

I knew I couldn't compete
with the unknown artist
so I resolved to copy
its shadow

I spun it dark and hairy
tinted it with dirt
Instead of crystalline threads, I used
strands of spit

My creation proved durable
Sunlight couldn't melt it
or rain wash it away
Its midnight beauty, jeweled
with dew and the wings of flies, fed
my mortal pride

The web trapped
bad dreams. Its skeins
slashed the wind, held strong
as love or hate

What snowflake could compete?

The Inquisitor of Snow

Day after day, the Grand Inquisitor of Snow
picks and scrapes at his scalp
as if it were a hotbed of heretics
crowning him with fire

He ruthlessly examines
each guilty prisoner-flake, pinching it
between his thumb and fingernail
tearing it apart
then flicking it to its fate

Oblivious to martyrdom,
the flakes snow down on ashtrays,
salt his scrambled eggs,
pepper spray Tolstoy's *War and Peace*
and speckle the world news

Unappeased by herbal balms
or prescription remedies, the Tormented One
scourges his scalp for years
till cities turn white,
savannas lie smothered,
the Himalayas grow taller
and after a roaring avalanche,
he mercifully disappears

Mai in December

White rose frost etches
the windowpanes of my classroom.
I explain S.A.D. syndrome to my students—
deprived of light
the body like a winter bulb
wants to sleep and sleep.

Mai sees through my lesson—
I'm tired beyond belief.
She offers to make me a shawl,
bring samples of bright yarn
so I can choose the colours.

All day long, the skeins
of my thoughts unwind,
a huge, crocheted snowflake
warms my back and shoulders,
melts fatigue from my bones.

Unfolding

I'm trying to make a paper snowflake
with graceful arms
    points like stars
perfect as the ones falling
past my classroom window

I've made them all my life but today
I can't fold the square properly
my friend's teenage son in a coma
    I fold the triangle point to point
fold again   *beaten senseless*
cut side to side but not quite through
    brain stem damaged   cut out the arms
but not too deep   *beaten
senseless* front and back from all sides
by who knows who

    Snowflakes
look the same but each one's different
like her boy and mine   turn
the triangle right side up   *which way is up*
    cut off the tip to make
a window at the center   *where's the centre
beaten senseless by who knows who*

unfold   *lying in a coma*
my snowflake's ugly   *holes like wounds*
    my students know why I can't concentrate
they take the scissors from my shaking hands
cut red and green snowflake constellations   *beaten
senseless*   what if it was my son?

My Address Book
for Margey

I haven't whited out her name
like first snow over a landscape

I've left her address intact
as though I could still knock on her door
and she'd open her arms—
we'd talk for hours
about everything we'd shared
during a lifetime of friendship
as I'd sample the shortbread cookies
baked for her seven grandchildren
her last Christmas on earth

Though she'll never write or call
I'll leave her among pages of the living
between the names of doctors
dentists, relatives
the emergency plumber and cancer hotline,
caterer and church.
I won't allow them to crowd her out
or push her off the page

Silence has its own voice
The Northern Lights play
across the sky like departed souls
trying to talk to us

I'll star her name to remind me
of where she'll always be—
 luminous on this page

The Ice Bee

I'm buying the icewine
because of the label.

Just want to pretend
I'm riding on that myth-sized bee
with moonlit stripes,
snowflakes lacing its wings.

Whisked across the winter sky
I'm Queen of the Night
drunk on the sight of Niagara vineyards.
There, growers and wine makers
who call themselves *Icebee*s
lift the nets protecting the vines
from ravenous birds
to harvest the grapes.

At my age, though
– cholesterol raging,
blood-sugar sky high –
I'm forbidden more than a few sips.

But each drop's a libation.

Like December grapes
suggesting the palate
of white-clover springtime,
honeydew summer,
autumn's apricot and apple scents,
I'll press my memories until

ice-tears squeeze out
and the sweetness remains,
full-bodied, rich.

As my bee and I cavort on wind
that billows my cloak,
rivers my hair,
I'll drink from a goblet and toast
my last season.
We'll pass earthly vineyards,
fly toward the spheres
humming like hinterland hives.

Icewine

He plucked my grapes in December
on the coldest night of the year.
No time to ferment feelings
or age them in mind-barrels.
His frosty eyes, biting
wind-fire tongue didn't believe
in cordial, candles or romance.
He got me drunk on apricot kisses
and the lychee tip of his sex.
I wanted to taste him with truffles
and sweet talk but he shoved
my manners aside to harvest
my full-bodied flavours.
I tried to safeguard my heart
by tying its vines to a fence
but he flew like a starving blackbird
to the last of my summertime.

The Alibis of Angels

The snow is telling lies,
whitening an alibi
we can touch, taste and swallow.
Seducing us, it leads us to believe
if we lie down and spread our arms
we will become angels.

The sky transforms us into fallen angels.
It teaches us to tell worn lies
as we whisper in each others' arms
bleaching alibis
we pretend to believe
but will never swallow.

Lovely as blue swallows
swooping like angels,
snow-feathers make us believe
we won't be frozen by the lies
and cozy alibis
blanketing our cache of arms.

Innocent and disarming
as winter swallows
sheltering in chimneys, we tuck alibis
around each other like guardian angels
watching over a bed of lies
only the gullible believe.

The snow is a blueness we now believe.
We shiver in each others' arms
as it fills our mouths with lies
that choke us when we swallow,
words like whitewashed angels
wrapping us in alibis.

Will we ever throw off the alibis that cache our arms?
Stop believing what can't be swallowed—
that we're both angels who never lie.

The Best Way to Eat a Snowflake

Say grace before you begin

then delicately
   as a butterfly
     dipping
her feet into nectar
  taste your way
    around
        and around
    the shape
of its divine pattern
      to preserve
the symmetry
  of that moment
    it tumbled
from the infinite
  on to your red mitten

When you reach
the very last hole
  at the centre
  of its being
melt your tongue inside it
tenderly as a lover

Snow

Whenever I reach orgasm, I've begun to snow. I snow an endless sky of needlepoint flakes like tiny cut-out stars falling peacefully on rooftops, muffling them in dreams. Snow on a carriage passing through a rowan forest and on to porcelain ladies dozing in their furs and cloaks lined with red velvet. Snow until the trees are lulled and I erase the imprints of the wheels and horses' hooves as they plod toward an inn with a crackling fire and down beds. My snowflakes smell of wood smoke, pine boughs, and everything else I touch as I snow across the centuries until I reach the green glass ball with the polar bear inside that I played with as a child. I shake it upside down and snow on the inverted sky and then on the river where I skated wearing my favourite angora mittens. I snow across my life to a field of Shetland ponies. Sparkle on their ragged coats and manes as they paw the icy crust for a mouthful of frozen grass. I even snow on myself as I call out their names, telling you that in the worst storms they burrow into drifts to keep warm, their breath rising like mist. I snow until there's no snow left, amazed I've made the world this beautiful.

A Little White Music

Out for my walk tonight
   snowflakes drift down
in fluffy
     whole notes
adagio then *andante*
   through the staves
of telephone wires
   the tines of tuning-fork twigs

Their flight uninterrupted
by rests or bar lines
they swish *sotto voce*
on a wind-silk breath

then as the tempo picks up
moderato, vivace, blizardo
they tango across the rooftops
and whistle in the trees

Blue
   for R.

The unicorn is blue but cannot speak
trapped inside a clear glass ball.
Shake his sky, the snow falls deep.

Outside his globe, the warm world sleeps
while he shivers in a winter shawl.
The unicorn is blue but cannot speak.

Beyond his sphere, the meadow-grass sweet,
there's a door to a forest where freedom calls.
Shake his sky, the snow falls deep.

Like the quarantined man who tries not to weep
behind the glass in the hospital hall,
the unicorn is blue but cannot speak.

Outside his circle, lovers meet.
The *mille fleurs* tapestry weaves them all.
Shake his sky, the snow falls deep.

Trapped in himself, his horn grows weak.
Will he find love to shatter his walls?
The unicorn is blue but cannot speak.
Shake his sky, the snow falls deep.

Old Stripper Snow

wears
    black lace
and torn fishnet stockings

She's baring herself
  on Toronto's streets
and there's nothing
    this sooty old girl
won't reveal
      as she sheds
  hair and teeth
    her once perfect skin
leaving behind
      cigarette butts
  chocolate bar wrappers
    a coat hanger
  gum-wads and globs of snot
we once horked at her

  Yes Old Stripper Snow
is doing her damnedest
  to leave showbiz
She's dancing her last
then slinking away
  to melt
off-scene in some urban park
    where she hopes
spring will stab her
with blades of green

April Snowman

His hat slumps on his shrunken head
    his scarf, a sodden string
One pebble-eye has fallen out
    his smile, a drooped quarter moon

Water slops down
   his slippery skin
    his belly
   caving in

I vow to cherish
   what's left of my life
before my own high noon

Distances

April puts out tentative shoots and tendrils
Let us begin with our fingertips

It's been a long time since I've slept beside you
I am uncertain what to do with my arms and legs

I try to lie beside you lightly as a leaf
Trace my contours and let your breath warm me

It's been months since my plane left your city
and I dreamt I tore off its wings

We approach like two solitary astronauts re-entering
the same space. Draw closer to me but not too close.

I have not lain beside you since the first snow fell
Do not sleep on the edge as if I were a cliff

Tomorrow is Easter

Snowdrops

fingerling
by
green
fingerling
snowdrops
unbutton
the
brown
bodice
of
spring

Hydrangeas

snowballs puffing up
a summer of green lapels—

boutonnieres gone wild

Hydrangeazzzzzz

wind-tossed
  sweet-smelling snowballs
    packed
with tiny white florets
and a blizzard
    of bees

Today People Are Snowing on Cabbagetown

This morning as on every Tuesday and Friday
somebody's loved ones are landing on rose beds
rooftops and newsstands   canopied sidewalk cafes
John Rachel Carlos Nancy Gustav Zelda
or who knows   No longer sick and afraid
they float toward porches and doormats
a second-hand bicycle shop
Bodies lighter than dried leaves
sift from sweet-smelling clouds
that drift from the old stone chimney
on the hem of historic St. James
Sunlight blessing my path
I remember my own dead at peace
Accepting that someday I too will snow down
I don't brush dark flakes from my sweater
I carry them willingly along
as I shop for red and green peppers
watch cats sunning in windows
on my way home down Parliament Street

End Notes:

So Many Words for Snow:

p.62 *composed by Malvin Franklin and Arthur Lange, 1908.
p.63 *a partially found poem from the L.L. Bean catalogue.
p.65 *Famous Blue Raincoat, by Leonard Cohen.
p.68 *Arachne competed with the goddess Athena to see who was the best weaver.
Though Arachne's tapestry was superior, Athena decreed that Arachne had lost the contest because she portrayed the gods disguised as animals.
p.72 *In Inuit mythology, the souls of the dead appear as the Northern Lights.

Acknowledgements (Kate Marshall Flaherty)

I would like to thank Richard Grove for his faith in my work, for making this collection possible, and for the great work he does in supporting Canadian poetry. I would also like to thank Donna Langevin and Deb Panko for the lovely journey we had together that brought about this book. Special thanks as well to my Muse and Plasticine workshop groups, who have keen eyes and kind hearts in editing poetry. My gratitude as well goes out to the Renaissance Conspiracy, Second Cup Poets and Hot Sauced Word poets, all of whom have shaped me as a poet and a person. As always I am indebted to Allan Briesmaster and Mick Burrs, who both continue to be inspirations and mentors. Many thanks to my friend and inspiration, Bernadette Peets, for her medicine wheel image for the section header. Last but not least, I am so grateful for my beloved families—the one I was born into and the one I gave birth to.

Versions of several poems, including "Gemini" and "Flight," first appeared in the manuscript entitled "Reaching V," edited by Mick Burrs.

Acknowledgements (Deb Panko)

Thank you Donna and Kate for your expert suggestions. Thank you Richard for publishing this book. Thank you to my late husband Ron for always being the first to hear my new poems.

Several poems have appeared in Cobourg's *Poetry'z Own* and in *Hola Cuba* by Hidden Brook Press.

Acknowledgements (Donna Langevin)

Heartfelt thanks to my publisher, Richard Grove for his continuing faith in me, and to Allan Briesmaster, James Comeaux, Deborah Panko, Kate Marshall-Flaherty, Kate Rogers, Richard Reinert and my fellow Art Bar workshoppers for much appreciated input. I would also like to thank Ron Cole for contributing his photo of the snowflake crocheted by his mother for my section header image.

Some of these poems have been published in *Poetry 'Own* and in my books, *The Second Language of Birds*, Hidden Brook Press, 2005, and *In the Café du Monde*, Hidden Brook Press, 2007. The poem "The Best Way to Eat a Snowflake" won first prize in the Cyclamens and Swords poetry contest in 2010.

All three of us are grateful to Ron Cole for his lovely cover image photo for *From O to Snow*, and to Thane Ladner for the wonderful bio photos.

About Kate Marshall Flaherty

Kate Marshall Flaherty is grateful to add *From O to Snow* to her other books of poetry, *where we are going*, *Hobbeldehoy*, *String of Mysteries* and *Tilted Equilibrium*. Her poetry has been published in journals such as *CV2, Descant, The Windsor Review, Quills, Ascent Aspirations, Other Voices, Saranac Review* and *Freefall*, and several Canadian and International Poetry Anthologies, including *Not A Muse*. She won first place in THIS Magazine's Great Canadian Literary Hunt, was short-listed for Descant's Best Canadian Poem, Nimrod's Pablo Neruda Poetry Prize, won first place twice for the Canadian Church Press Awards, and won honorable mentions for CV2's 48-hour poetry contest and the GritLIT Literary Awards. Kate has participated for four years now in the annual National Random Acts of Poetry several times, where she "poemed" unsuspecting people in hospitals, cafes, parks, libraries, and on the street. She lives with her family in Toronto where she teaches yoga and guides teen retreats on the Golden Rule. Poetry is her life-line.

About Deborah Panko

Deborah Panko retired early from teaching English at the Toronto District School Board and moved east, feeling fortunate to have settled in lovely Cobourg with the Northumberland Hills, Presqu'le Park and big city Toronto all within easy reach. She takes time to walk, watch birds, ride her bike, enjoy a wealth of arts events, play piano, read (especially the classics), travel and be with family and friends. Hidden Brook Press published her first book of poetry, *Somewhat Elsewhere*, in 2008.

Deborah   Donna   Katie

About Donna Langevin

Donna Langevin lives in Toronto. She is a retired ESL teacher and the co-author of five texts. Her poems have appeared in numerous journals such as the *Antigonish Review, Arc* and *Descant*. She won the 2004 Ray Burrell Award for Poetry, second prize, first prize in the 2008 Ontario Poetry Society Spring Contest, and first prize in the 2009 Cyclamens and Swords contest. Her books of poetry include *The Second Language of Birds*, Hidden Brook Press, 2005, and *In the Café du Monde*, Hidden Brook Press, 2007, and two chapbooks, *Songbirds of the Hours*, Fooliar Press, 2005 and *The Middle-aged Man in the Sea*, Lyricalmyrical Press, 2009. She prefers to write about snow than to live in it, so she spends a lot of time visiting her mother in sunny New Orleans.

Other Hidden Brook Press books by these authors.

Kate Marshall Flaherty
Tilted Equilibrium
1-894553-70-5
String of Mysteries
978-1-897475-10-2

Deborah Panko
Somewhat Elsewhere
978-1-897475-13-3

Donna Langevin
The Second Language of Birds
1-894553-61-6
In the Café du Monde
978-1-897475-03-4

All of these books are available via
www.HiddenBrookPress.com

www.ingramcontent.com/pod-product-compliance
Lightning Source LLC
Chambersburg PA
CBHW071403080526
44587CB00017B/3164